The Really **Wild Life** of **Birds** of **Prey**™

GREAT HORNED OWLS

DOUG WECHSLER
THE ACADEMY OF NATURAL SCIENCES

The Rosen Publishing Group's
PowerKids Press™
New York

For Doug Emery, who shared so many incredible adventures with me.

About the Author
Wildlife biologist, ornithologist, and photographer Doug Wechsler has studied birds, snakes, frogs, and other wildlife around the world. Doug Wechsler works at The Academy of Natural Sciences of Philadelphia, a natural history museum. As part of his job, he travels to rain forests and remote parts of the world to take pictures of birds. He has taken part in expeditions to Ecuador, the Philippines, Borneo, Cuba, Cameroon, and many other countries.

Published in 2001 by The Rosen Publishing Group, Inc.
29 East 21st Street, New York, NY 10010

First Edition

Book Design: Michael de Guzman

Photo Credits: Doug Wechsler portrait by Bruce Hallett; pp. 4, 7 © A. & S. Carey/VIREO; p. 8 © W. Greene/VIREO; p. 11 © J. Heidecker/VIREO; p. 12 © Steven Holt/VIREO; p. 15 © Sam Fried/VIREO; p. 16 © R. Day/VIREO; p. 19© F. Truslow/VIREO; . 20 © John Cancalosi/VIREO; p. 22 © T. J. Ulrich/VIREO.
All photographs from VIREO (Visual Resources for Ornithology), The Academy of Natural Sciences' worldwide collection of bird photographs.

Wechsler, Doug.
    Great Horned Owls / by Doug Wechsler.
       p. cm.— (The really wild life of birds of prey)
    Summary: Describes the physical characteristics, behavior, and habitat of the great horned owl.
    ISBN 0-8239-5599-0 (lib. bdg. : alk. paper)
    1. Great horned owl—Juvenile literature. [1. Great horned owl. 2. Owls.] I. Title.

QL696.S83 W43 2000
598.9'7—dc21
                                                                 99-044084

CONTENTS

THE EVERYWHERE OWL

You have probably heard the great horned owl's hoot in movies about the Wild West. If you have walked in the woods beneath pine trees, chances are you have passed nearby one. The great horned owl is one of the largest owls. It can weigh as much as five pounds (2.3 kg). Great horned owls are found just about everywhere in North America except in the **arctic tundra**. They also live in many different areas of South America. They live in deserts, grasslands, and at the edge of woods. They also live in large city parks and on farms. Almost any type of **habitat** will do as long as there is plenty of food and a place to hide.

A great horned owl can live in many different habitats, such as snowy forests or dry deserts.

Great horned owls are good fliers, but they are not as swift as some other birds of **prey**. Instead they use **stealth**. This means that they fly silently to sneak up on their prey. If you look at the feather on the front edge of an owl wing, you will see how owls keep quiet. The feather is a little fluffy, and has soft **bristles** on its front edge. The other feathers on the wing are also soft. The soft feathers silence the "whoosh" sound that the air makes against the wing. A great horned owl's prey hears nothing as the owl swoops in. The stealthy owl can hear its prey as it flies in to make the kill.

An owl's soft, quiet feathers help it make sneak attacks on its prey.

DOUG SAYS

GREAT HORNED OWLS GET THEIR NAME FROM THE HORNLIKE TUFTS, OR BUNCHES OF FEATHERS, ABOVE THEIR EARS.

WHO HOOTS, "HOO HOO-HOOO HOOO HOOO?"

Snow is falling in the woods. You hear five deep hoots, "hoo hoo-hooo hooo hooo." Seven higher-pitched hoots answer, "hoo hoo-hoo hooo hoo-hoo hooo." You are listening to a pair of great horned owls singing a **duet**. The male has a gruff, deep voice. The female's voice is higher. She also adds a couple of extra hoots. The calling keeps the pair in touch with one another. Great horned owls call most in winter before nesting. They also call to tell other great horned owls, "This is our **territory**. We live here. Stay away."

The male great horned owl has a gruff and deep hoot. A female owl has a higher-pitched sound with extra hoots.

WHAT BIG EYES YOU HAVE!

If your eyes were like an owl's, they would be the size of tennis balls. The big eyes of an owl help it to hunt at night. Our eyes are shaped like globes. An owl's eyes are more pear-shaped. They work like small **telescopes**. They help owls see well at night. The backs of their eyes are packed with cells called **rods**. Rods are very good at detecting dim light. Rods send messages to the brain. The brain uses the messages to form a black-and-white picture in the owl's mind. We have rods, too, but we have more of the cells, called **cones**. Cones help us see color. Owls do not have many cones, but colors do not show up in the dark anyway.

An owl's huge eyes take up a lot of space in its skull.

DOUG SAYS

GREAT HORNED OWLS HAVE FEW NATURAL ENEMIES.

A NECK THAT TURNS HALF WAY AROUND!

An owl's eyes are in the front of its head, like our eyes are. Owls cannot move their eyes like we can. How does an owl see to the side or behind itself? An owl can turn its neck more than half way around. It can face backward to see what is going on behind it. An owl can quickly turn its head to see prey or enemies.

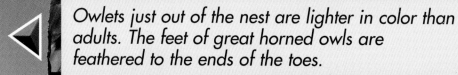

Owlets just out of the nest are lighter in color than adults. The feet of great horned owls are feathered to the ends of the toes.

THE MENU

When a great horned owl is hungry, what does it eat? An owl eats almost any small animal. Great horned owls are not picky eaters. They eat mostly small mammals such as rabbits, squirrels, mice, and gophers. When **waterfowl** are available they eat ducks and **coots**. The great horned owl gulps down all but its largest prey whole. It is also one of the few animals that eat skunks.

Great horned owls eat rabbits, squirrels, waterfowl, mice, reptiles, fish, and even other owls.

WHERE DO THE GULPED GOPHERS GO?

After gulping a gopher, the great horned owl **digests** it in its stomach. The digested food goes into the **intestine**. After 16 hours, all that is left in the stomach is hair and bones. The owl gets rid of the hair and bones by coughing them up. Out comes a neat package of hair and bones. You can collect these owl pellets beneath a **roost** tree. If you carefully tear the pellet apart, you will find a little skull. The pattern and shape of the teeth in the skull tells you it was a gopher.

Young owlets easily swallow mice and rats whole.

Owls do not know the first thing about building a nest. Instead they look for an old hawk nest, a cliff ledge, or a broken treetop. A great horned owl's favorite nest is the old stick nest of a red-tailed hawk.

Great horned owls start to nest in winter. They can keep their eggs warm even when the temperature is -25° **Fahrenheit** (-32° C). The female spends almost all of her time in the nest. She rarely leaves until the young are old enough to keep warm on their own. The male brings all the food. Five mice or one rabbit might be a night's meal.

Great horned owls nest in many different kinds of places. They can even nest on the ground.

THE OWLETS HATCH

Owlets start to make noise even before they hatch. They come out of the egg with their eyes closed. The female only lays one egg every two days. The oldest owlets, or the ones born earliest, are the biggest. If there is not enough food, the oldest owlets will grab all the food and the youngest will starve. This way, even in years when food is hard to find, at least one owlet may **survive**.

Great horned owls usually have two or three young, but they can raise as many as five.

TRACKING AN OWL

Here is a special tip on finding great horned owls. Listen to the crows! If crows find an owl in the daytime, they "caw" loudly. The noisy crows take turns diving at the owl. When the owl flies, the cawing gets louder. The crows follow the owl and bother it even more. The crows lose interest only when the owl finds a good place to hide. The owl may hide in the thick top of an evergreen tree. Sometimes, if you follow cawing crows, they will lead you to a red-tailed hawk or a cat instead of an owl. Though great horned owls are common across North America, you may have to look hard to see one!

GLOSSARY

arctic tundra (AR-tik TUN-druh) Land with grasses, low-growing plants, and no trees near the northern edge of North America, Europe, and Asia.

bristles (BRIH-selz) Short, stiff, hairlike fibers.

cones (KOHNZ) Special cells in the back of the eyes that spot colors.

coots (KOOTZ) Blackish duck-sized waterbirds with cone-shaped white beaks.

digests (dy-JESTS) When the body breaks down food to use for energy.

duet (DOO-et) Two singers performing together.

Fahrenheit (FEHR-un-hyt) A kind of temperature scale that measures the freezing point of water as 32 degrees and the boiling point as 212 degrees.

habitat (HA-bih-tat) The surroundings where an animal lives.

intestine (in-TES-tin) The part of the digestive system that extends below the stomach.

owlets (OW-lets) Young owls that cannot fly yet.

prey (PRAY) An animal that is eaten by another animal for food.

rods (RODS) Special cells in the back of the eye that detect faint light.

roost (ROOST) A place where birds sleep.

stealth (STELTH) Done in a secret, sneaky way.

survive (sur-VYV) To stay alive.

telescopes (TEL-uh-skohps) Instruments used to make distant objects appear closer and bigger.

territory (TEHR-uh-TOHR-ee) Land or space that is controlled by a person or an animal.

waterfowl (WAT-er-fowl) Ducks, geese, swans, and similar waterbirds.

INDEX

WEB SITES

To learn more about great horned owls, check out these Web sites:

http://www.id.blm.gov/bopnca/index.html
http://www.raptor.cvm.umn.edu
http://www.acnatsci.org/vireo (Readers can order a raptor slide set.)